Affiliate Marketing

The Comprehensive Manual for Achieving High Sales
and Commencing an Lucrative E-commerce Venture

(A Comprehensive Handbook on Constructing a
Lucrative Affiliate Enterprise)

Matthew Labrie

TABLE OF CONTENT

Enhancing Your Product With Affiliate Marketing

To enhance your product in affiliate marketing, follow these necessary steps:

Assess the product/service you endorse—When promoting your offerings, ensure to write a review for each. A typical review consists of one page and includes the following details:

• Name of product, service, or website

• Product, service, or website described briefly

Where to buy or access the item.

Positive aspects of the product

Drawbacks - Product dislikes

• Is the price fair, too high, or too low?

Do you recommend this product and to whom?

• No further remarks.

• Provide owner's contact details.

To receive products for your blog reviews, there are two methods available.

a) Sign up for a blog review network— Fill out a form with your blog and personal details. Do it, receive review invitations. You choose the ones you accept and the ones you decline. If you agree, you typically receive a product, which becomes yours. You use it and then write a review. At times, along with the product, you can receive nominal compensation such as a gift card or sweepstakes entry.

Here are some networks to consider:

Sponsored Reviews - Effective for attracting honest product reviewers. They are motivated by the opportunity to make money.

If you join for free, you may have an opportunity to connect with a PR company at Prizey.

MomSelect is a review network for bloggers and non-bloggers.

You can't choose the invitations you receive with blog networks. You may have a technology-focused blog that interests you. You want to test out quality products before becoming an affiliate, but you might receive invitations for dish detergent or shampoo instead. Sure, you are welcome to decline. However, accepting and reviewing their products allows you to practice writing reviews for the products you do plan to affiliate with. Growing your audience is crucial, and they assist in accomplishing this goal. This is an excellent method for beginner bloggers to boost site traffic.

b) Request them—Locate the desired company to be affiliated with. Inquire if they'd send a desired product for review and potential promotion on your site. Introduce yourself and your blog briefly. Crafting a clear and persuasive inquiry requires effort, but the end result is valuable.

Make sure to accept products you truly believe in. If you wouldn't pay $100 for jeans, decline the invitation. You will struggle to persuade another person to purchase them. You would face challenges in promoting them on your site as an affiliate.

Make a video tutorial to demonstrate the usage of the product/service—Video tutorials effectively explain practical topics. You can demonstrate to your audience and provide them with a visual representation for a clearer comprehension of the product/service functioning.

Follow these steps to prepare a good video tutorial:

a) Create a script: Pick a concept or short task you can explain briefly. Make it about 300 words as videos should ideally be three to five minutes long. Write the script to resemble a conversation. Carefully read and physically demonstrate the steps multiple times. Highlighting action cues in your script when viewing it on a monitor aids in maintaining focus and staying on task for the video.

b) Formulate a simulation—Choose the type of content, occurrence, or tasks you wish to display and execute it. Ensure its functionality and demonstrate its simplicity. Ensure your actions align with the script by practicing it multiple times.

c) Capture the simulation and narration—Preferably in three steps.

Use one monitor for recording your script and another for the simulation. It's okay if you slightly deviate from your script, don't worry. That's normal when you're trying to have a casual conversation. Maintain a natural tone, but concentrate on mimicking. Experience a clear, seamless screen display. Using a touchpad mouse is not recommended for computer simulations. The movements may be abrupt. Opt for a standard mouse and move it seamlessly. Avoid

Talking and moving the mouse together makes editing difficult.

• Re-record the audio—Separate it from the video. Reread your script. Ensure you pause where necessary. For this voiceover, be mindful of pitch variation, avoid repetitive rhymes, enunciate clearly with confidence, and vary your speaking pace for a natural sound.

• Sync the timing—Play both tracks simultaneously after re-recording the audio. Match the timing. Don't fret if your pauses don't align precisely. You can vary the distance between audio waves and approach.

Post-process simulation by removing unnecessary long pauses and moments of inaction in the audio. You can place callouts to highlight important elements on the screen. Title slide: keep it to about two seconds in your video. Ensure it conveys the video's purpose. Crossfade the recording with the title.

The software you use affects callouts, annotations, and animation options. Ensure maximum simplicity. More additions to your video equal a larger file size. Larger file sizes result in longer production times. Visit istockaudio.com to discover a suitable loop or sting for your music integration.

Convert the video to MP4 format and incorporate it. Then transfer it to your server. Uploading it to YouTube will trigger automatic HD rendering. HD ensures clear, non-blurry text visibility. YouTube's voice recognition software automatically syncs captions with the voice. Upload the script in the captions section. The auto-sync program aids non-native speakers and individuals with hearing difficulties in understanding the content of your video.

Search engine optimization is also enhanced.

Promote it on your website or blog—Maximize the tutorial's visibility. Recall the importance of high-quality content. Engage and excite your audience to increase their site visits and session duration.

Remember the quality rule when choosing your products. Many bloggers neglect product quality when making selections. They just promote anything. Sometimes they promote quality merchandise, but lack concern for how they promote it. They always use the same old method to promote products. Consider the vendor, please. They prioritize both customers and integrity. Poor promotion of their products doesn't make them look good.

That's why video tutorials are popular. They provide a fresh perspective on existing products or an initial perspective on new products. Delivering valuable content helps establish trust with your audience.

Social media is the powerful medium for connecting with the masses. All aspiring affiliate marketers must engage with many individuals. Social media sites can assist you. Affiliate marketers can harness the power of social media. Social media platforms enable users to connect and share opinions with diverse individuals.

Social media can aid in achieving affiliate marketing success. They include:

• Promote affiliate programs to your followers, allowing them to share your posts and links. You can advertise the products you are affiliated with through posts and blogs on your page. You can also create fan pages to enhance your promotion.

• Connect with your audience—Expand your network by adding like-minded individuals who will value your message. Improved audience coordination can be achieved through the formation of interactive groups. After sharing the information about your affiliate products, request audience feedback. Feedback is crucial for audience connection and strategic adjustments. Inform them about your affiliate products and seek feedback.

Stay informed—Stay updated on market happenings. Social media reveals new product launches and public preferences. This will assist you in understanding current trends and refining your affiliate marketing strategies effectively.

Competition is fierce among affiliate marketers due to the high number of participants. Here are some social media tips to gain a market advantage.

• Emphasize connections—Facebook, Google, and Twitter are social media platforms. Emphasize the term 'social.' Ensure connecting with the right individuals and foster positive relationships with them. Consider a fan page without numbering. This will increase your knowledge. Fostering strong client relationships aids promotion. They'll want to share your message with friends on their page.

Include social bookmarking—Place a social bookmarking button on your site. Next, request your visitors to follow. If your posts are liked by visitors, it is easy for them to share. Social bookmarking is free, so make use of it.

Blog wiser, not harder – Some bloggers exert much effort and invest countless hours into creating blogs that receive minimal exposure. Blog smart when creating your site's posts. The primary goal is to captivate the visitor's attention. Provide informative, valuable data promptly. This action will boost your social media presence.

These tips are crucial for enhancing your online presence. Mastering social media will simplify the process of discovering and engaging potential clients. Once you've selected the appropriate products/services, be completely truthful and transparent with potential customers. Through social media, you can win their hearts.

Many bloggers don't think they can earn from email marketing, so they avoid using it. They are blind to the benefits. They believe it's not worth their time, so they don't attempt it. To know what a new restaurant is like, you must try it.

You might be forgoing something amazing.

Don't overlook important factors as a blogger, as they can later be realized as mistakes. Things to know before starting your email marketing campaign:

• Increase your subscriber count—You want to maximize the number of subscribers on your list. Your email would receive blog-like traffic. Your subscribers equal your traffic in email marketing. Greater blog traffic yields superior outcomes. Email and subscribers are identical. Greater results come with more possessions.

• Lack of originality in emails is a common mistake in email marketing. This method efficiently prompts subscribers to unsubscribe. If your emails lack original, valuable content, people will unsubscribe quickly. They desire an uncluttered inbox.

Write to demonstrate your familiarity with the product—Avoid using pre-written reviews taken directly from advertisements. Readers desire a sense of your expertise. They want a personal touch that demonstrates product knowledge. If possible, ask for the item and test it beforehand. You gain direct experience to share with your reader. In this manner, you will have an enhanced ability to address any inquiries from your readers regarding the products.

• Be truthful in your reviews—Not all products are exceptional. If something is just average, simply state it. You can rate your reviews with a numerical scale from 1 to 5. Make sure to rate it according to your judgment.

• Avoid excessive use of links—Using links is important, but having five links on the same keyword in the first paragraph is unnecessary. Be more creative and effective with your links to limit their number. Use customized graphical banners that clearly indicate the content of the link, such as "Learn more about the product," "View the product," or "Checkout my review." These captivate readers and heighten their product interest.

Choosing A Niche

Any subjects of personal interest or topics that you wish to endorse, preferably within the evergreen niches such as dating, online income generation, human sexuality, personal development, business strategies, technology advancements, health improvement, and weight management, among others.

This is a critical juncture where many individuals encounter difficulty: the initial stage in selecting a niche. In the event of any potential misconceptions, it is important to note that a niche refers to a compact, yet well-defined market. Consider a niche as a distinct classification or domain. A selection of niches would entail

Canine obedience instruction, body mass reduction, or wanderlust. These are all relatively comprehensive illustrations, which will aid in comprehending the given concept. Typically, one would seek to identify a specialized sub-niche, such as 'dog training specifically tailored for Alsations'.

Sub-niches such as 'weight reduction for individuals with diabetes' or 'travel for individuals with backpacking preferences' exhibit a lower level of competition when compared to their broader niche counterparts.

Choosing A Niche

One should seek out a product or service that caters to individuals' needs, enhancing their quality of life, resolving specific challenges they encounter, or enhancing their well-being or appearance. Certain individuals often err by serendipitously encountering a product, service, or idea that they presume will universally appeal, subsequently endeavoring to establish a market for it even when one does not exist. Adhere to products or services that cater to the preferences of the target audience. There exist certain market segments that will consistently generate profits, commonly referred to as the "

Persistently relevant categories encompassing health, physical fitness, body management, self-improvement, technological advancements, online income generation, interpersonal relationships, and human sexuality. There will consistently be a demand for these products. Fortunately, there is a multitude of subcategories present within these primary categories, comprising an extensive array of new merchandise and services entering the market on a daily basis, providing ample opportunities for you to capitalize upon. Consider all the novel technological devices, dietary trends, and online marketing offerings available in the market.

Methods for Discovering a Specialized Market

In order to effectively explore and investigate new market niches, I employ several strategies. Firstly, I ensure that I remain informed about the latest trends and popular subjects by regularly perusing newspapers, magazines, blogs, and participating in discussion forums. Additionally, I stay updated by closely following news broadcasts and monitoring the prevailing topics on social media platforms such as Twitter and Facebook. If I were inclined to explore the weight loss niche, I would peruse weight loss forums and blogs, seeking chat rooms dedicated to discussions on weight loss and diets. Engaging in conversations with individuals therein, I would gather information about the latest supplements and dietary regimens they are employing to achieve their health objectives.

Generate potential resolutions to your predicaments.

Another approach that I adhere to involves contemplating the quandaries or predicaments I encounter in my daily existence, seeking potential solutions through the identification of products or services that may prove beneficial. Alternatively, I will endeavor to juxtapose two distinct interests that appeal to me, such as baseball and coffee, in order to ascertain if a niche can be identified.

They are ready to be capitalized upon... coffee mugs adorned with depictions of baseball players! Though it may seem whimsical, the profitability of such merchandise is rather astonishing. You will find it truly astonishing/astounding/surprising.

quantity of concepts you are capable of generating.

Please utilize search engines such as Google, Yahoo, and social platforms like Twitter, as well as e-commerce websites like eBay and Amazon.

In a more formal tone, you could say: "To be more precise, I conduct assessments using Google Hot Trends, Yahoo Buzz, Twitter trending, eBay Pulse, and the top-selling items on Amazon." These exhibits demonstrate the prevailing trends and provide me with novel concepts that would have never crossed my mind otherwise. In addition, I peruse online platforms that offer merchandise, assessing their sales performance and evaluating customer feedback.

By following any of the aforementioned steps diligently, I assure you that in under one hour you will have compiled an extensive catalogue of potential niche markets to examine. Ensure that you meticulously record all the ideas that arise. The subsequent stage I undertake is 'conducting keyword research', a crucial step within this comprehensive process that will enable us to determine the viability of exploring these niches.

Bonus: Goal Wizard

In gratitude for your readership of this book, I would like to extend to you a complimentary resource I have designed, which I believe will prove beneficial in your pursuit of affiliate marketing. The complimentary resource is referred to as the Goal Wizard. My standard fee for access is typically $27, however, I am providing it to you at no cost in exchange for reading this book.

At its fundamental essence, The Goal Wizard serves as a standardized template. However, once the form is completed, the wizard employs its enchantment, facilitating the process of dissecting your aspirations from seemingly insurmountable objectives into manageable, pragmatic actions.

The most challenging aspect of any objective lies in the absence of a clear roadmap, rendering it seemingly unattainable. An effective approach to address this challenge is to employ reverse engineering techniques, wherein one analyzes their major objective and develops a series of actionable steps that can be followed chronologically to progress from the current state to the desired goal.

The objective in affiliate marketing typically centers around achieving financial independence to replace a conventional full-time job, wherein one can generate sufficient income to sustain oneself, support their family, and partake in social activities, devoid of the limitations imposed by financial constraints or lack of time. It is important to cultivate a well-rounded personal life beyond one's professional commitments. An unconventional notion in the present era, yet a pursuit that should be embraced by all.

To achieve this ambitious objective, it is imperative to ascertain the precise financial target required for its fulfillment.

It is not sufficient to simply state, "I desire to attain wealth in order to have leisure time" or "I aspire to be affluent so that I can allocate more time with my family and engage in personal interests." Moreover, an indeterminate quantity cannot be deemed suitable in this context. It would be deemed inappropriate to assert, "I require one million dollars as that is commensurate with the wealth of affluent individuals."

While it is a universal desire to possess a substantial sum of one million dollars, it is plausible that a lower amount could sufficiently sustain an individual's envisioned way of life. Perhaps if one maintains a lavish lifestyle, a greater sum may be necessary. However, it is imperative to ascertain the exact monetary figure required to achieve one's objective.

In order to ascertain this particular, ambitious target amount, it is necessary to itemize all your expenditures in life, along with any additional expenses required for an ideal standard of living. After obtaining a specific quantity, it can subsequently be incorporated into your overarching objective within the Goal Wizard.

Now that you have established the designated monthly target amount, you can proceed to dissect it into practical and feasible actions.

Therefore, the initial phase of analysis involves dividing the task into two primary actions that will facilitate the attainment of the desired financial outcome. In the realm of affiliate marketing, these activities encompass the establishment of a blog as well as the creation of a YouTube channel, both of which serve to endorse and propagate the content of your blog.

Now, it is necessary to further deconstruct these objectives into an additional level of simplicity. Merely stating phrases such as 'I desire a website' or 'I wish to engage in blogging' lacks the depth and specificity required. You must perform a comprehensive analysis to delineate the desired levels of website traffic, the number of ranking pages, and the targeted keyword search volume in order to ascertain the exact magnitude of traffic generation. I require a significant number of subscribers on the YouTube platform. It is probable that I would require a sufficient number of instructive videos in order to secure a comparable number of subscribers."

Subsequently, in the final phase of dissecting your objective, it is imperative to establish concrete, incremental, strategic, and practicable measures that can be implemented.

What methods do you employ to obtain subscribers? Perhaps you should consider creating a video on a weekly or daily basis.

What strategies will you employ to generate a substantial volume of traffic to your website, thereby increasing the potential for a significant number of clicks on your affiliate offer, consequently yielding a substantial monetary outcome? You must analyze and deconstruct the specific measures you intend to undertake.

In this instance, you are generating traffic by means of YouTube. However, what additional measures must be undertaken to effectively generate that traffic? Would you be interested in enrolling in a instructional program designed to enhance your knowledge and skills in optimizing the ranking of YouTube videos? What approach will you employ to conduct keyword research for YouTube content?

The essence lies in the process of dissecting an apparently insurmountable and elusive primary objective into manageable and executable increments. After employing the Goal Wizard, this seemingly unattainable goal will appear much less formidable.

It is highly precise and easily quantifiable. And you possess the capability to accomplish the task at hand. As you are now aware of the necessary course of action.

Avoiding Common Errors In Affiliate Marketing.

As the handbook nears its conclusion and concludes its distribution, it is imperative to be aware of the cautionary indicators and treacherous territory that should be avoided within the realm of affiliate marketing.

Please adjust the tuning of your device...

Affiliate marketing is widely regarded as a highly effective and lucrative method for generating income on the internet. This program offers each individual an opportunity to generate a profit via the Internet. Given their ease of access, operational simplicity, and reliable commission structure, an increasing number of individuals are now expressing their willingness to engage in these affiliate marketing programs.

Nevertheless, akin to all enterprises, the realm of affiliate marketing encompasses numerous pitfalls. Making some of the most prevalent errors could result in a significant deduction from the daily earnings of advertisers. It is more advantageous to refrain from associating with them, rather than experiencing regret later on.

Mistake number one: Selecting an unsuitable affiliate.

Numerous individuals have a pressing need to swiftly engage in affiliate marketing. In their eagerness to attain significance, they frequently gravitate towards transient trends. These are the types of items that the program considers to be "trending." They choose the item based on its popularity without adequately considering whether it fulfills their specific needs. This decision clearly lacks strategic acumen.

Instead of following that passing trend, endeavor to choose an item that truly captures your interest. In order for any endeavor to achieve success, it is imperative to allocate sufficient space for strategic planning and the efficient organization of activities.

Select an item that appeals to your preferences. Subsequently, engage in a thorough examination of the product to ascertain its level of popularity. Promoting a product or idea you are deeply passionate about is more straightforward compared to promoting one solely for financial gain.

Error number two: Engaging in excessive participation in affiliate programs.

Given the straightforward nature of joining affiliate programs, one may be enticed to enroll in multiple affiliate programs to maximize their potential for income generation. Apart from the possibility of perceiving oneself as benefiting greatly and having nothing to risk by assuming a crucial role in certain affiliate programs.

Indeed, that is an exceptional approach to generate diverse streams of income. However, by participating in multiple projects and striving to advance them concurrently, your ability to concentrate on each individual endeavor will be impeded.

The outcome? The true potential of your affiliate program remains largely unexplored, and consequently, the resulting revenue may not meet the initial expectations as anticipated. To achieve optimal results, it is advisable to exclusively participate in a program that offers a minimum commission rate of 40%. Subsequently, exert maximum dedication as you vigorously promote your products. Once you ascertain that it is generating a discernible profit, you may consider enrolling in another affiliate program at that juncture.

The approach entails proceeding in a gradual manner. There exists a genuine imperative to refrain from hastiness, especially when it comes to the domain of affiliate marketing. Given the current state of affairs, the prospects ahead appear exceedingly favorable, indicating that the long-term viability of affiliate marketing is assured.

Error number three: Failing to acknowledge the item or make use of the offered assistance.

As an affiliate, your primary objective is to effectively and convincingly promote a product or service and attract customers. In order for you to achieve this objective, it is imperative that you possess the ability to effectively convey and offer that particular product and service to the customers. It is therefore quite difficult for you to accomplish this task given that, ultimately, you have not

Having made an attempt at these things. Hence, you will fail to effectively promote and propose them. You will also fail to stimulate a desire in your customers to avail themselves of any of the products or services you are marketing.

Prior to becoming an affiliate, it is recommended to firsthand sample the product or service to verify its efficacy in meeting the stated promises. If, by any chance, you have actually done so, you are among those credible individuals who possess firsthand knowledge of both the merits and drawbacks associated with it. Subsequently, your clientele will discern the sincerity and integrity within you, thereby motivating them to engage in their own endeavors.

Numerous affiliate advertisers have made these mistakes and are now facing the consequences of their actions. In order to avoid experiencing similar circumstances, it is advisable to make every effort to prevent repeating the same mistakes.

Time is the key. Allocate time to thoroughly evaluate your marketing system and ascertain whether it is functioning optimally. When executed correctly, you will be able to enhance your affiliate marketing program and realize greater profits.

Five Approaches to Assessing a Product or Service

As a member of the affiliated party, this is the paramount element of the procedure. It is futile to analyze the intricacies of an affiliate program unless you discover a product that you can ascertain your visitors will purchase.

1. Does the product or service align with the content and purpose of your site or page?

The presence of financial service banners on a beauty website appears incongruous. If you are employed as an affiliate, such commingling solely serves to divert the attention of the visitor.

2. Does the website of the company exhibit an attractive design and optimal functionality?

The company's website should exude a captivating appeal while maintaining a profound level of professionalism. We can infer limited potential in websites that exhibit broken links and exhibit challenging navigation. Do not refer your visitors to websites of inferior quality, as this can potentially compromise your reputation.

3. Do the offerings of the program encompass high-quality products and services available at reasonable price points?

As a seller, it is imperative to maintain confidence in the products or services you offer. If your familiarity with the product is lacking, how can you effectively promote it? Furthermore, it is imperative to ascertain that the pricing of the products is both fair and reasonable.

4. Acquire and evaluate the products that you intend to endorse.

It is highly advisable to procure a majority of the products you are endorsing. Possessing direct personal experience with a particular item provides you with a competitive edge over other affiliates who are marketing the identical product. Assuming a commission rate of 25%, the breakeven point can be attained by making a minimum of four sales.

5. Does the company offer exemplary customer service?

This holds significance, albeit without direct relevance to you. Customers of the affiliate program may forward emails to you due to the company's lack of response to their inquiries. Regrettably, there is indeed nothing within your control regarding this situation. You may consider forwarding their request using the provided email and contact information. However, it is important to bear in mind that any failure to achieve the desired outcome could be attributed to you and your business.

The majority of individuals aspire to assume the role of an entrepreneur and have complete control over their own professional endeavors. The advent of the Internet has enabled countless individuals to turn their aspirations into tangible achievements. However, I would venture to say that amidst every accomplished affiliate, there likely exist countless individuals who have endeavored but ultimately met with failure. There is an abundance of affiliate marketing ideas available on the Internet; nevertheless, adhering to the subsequent three affiliate marketing recommendations will shield you from becoming a victim of the numerous scams prevalent within the realm of 'home based business opportunities'.

What makes affiliate programs highly appealing?

The primary benefits offered by online entrepreneurship include emancipation from hierarchical control, adaptable work arrangements, and the potential to amass substantial fortunes while operating from the convenience of one's personal abode. Although the allure of freedom and autonomy may be considerable, it is important to note that a significant majority of affiliates remain unaware of the fact that approximately 90% of newly established businesses experience failure within the initial year. My intention is not to dissuade or demoralize, but rather to caution you regarding the practicalities associated with generating income online. Anyone can get into online business as it involves very little start-up costs, and there are many wonderful affiliate programs. Additionally, a plethora of advantageous concepts and strategies exist in the realm of affiliate marketing that can aid in initiating your online presence. Regrettably, there is a significant likelihood of failure. It is imperative to exercise caution when selecting the programs and products for investment.

Three Key Affiliate Marketing Strategies for Safeguarding Against Online Fraudulent Activities

Fortunately, it is indeed feasible to earn a respectable income through online means. Regrettably, we reside in an era characterized by increasingly sophisticated instances of fraudulent activities conducted through online businesses. If you believe that your investment in your online business is minimal, reconsider this notion. It is imperative to acknowledge that your commitment extends beyond monetary resources, encompassing your time, vitality, and cognitive attentiveness. Prudent discernment of your investments is crucial to prevent potential drain on these valuable assets within this enterprise. The subsequent affiliate marketing concepts will provide you with a preliminary understanding of the indicative indicators of fraudulent practices within online commerce:

Conduct an Information Search or Research

If you encounter any difficulty in locating relevant information pertaining to a specific affiliate program or product, it is advisable to be cautious and remain vigilant. Reputable affiliate programs will undoubtedly possess a documented history that you can uncover. Therefore, refrain from succumbing to the allure of purchasing the recently released "push-button traffic generation software." Regardless of the temporary 'massive discount' they are currently offering, it would be advisable to exercise patience and observe the product's presence and substantiated claims over a period of at least six months. Subsequently, you may contemplate the purchase.

Ask For Testimonials

The majority of product recommendation landing pages feature an image displaying an 'income sheet', showcasing a monthly revenue of $10,000. This is intended to demonstrate the purported efficacy of the product or program. Furthermore, the majority of landing pages do not expound upon the methods they employ to generate substantial monetary gains. It will be formulated with 'confidential' language that conceals the true nature of the product. Thus, it is advisable not to succumb to such deceitful tactics. Alternatively, please verify the authenticity of testimonials. No, I am referring to the ones they have published on their official website. (Considering the possibilities of any source of information). Kindly reach out to them to obtain the precise names and addresses of individuals whom you may contact to inquire about the program's impact on their respective businesses. You may also consider conducting a Google search to find authentic user reviews. If you conduct a thorough search using the keywords "XYZ scam," there is a high likelihood that you will uncover any negative information pertaining to the particular product or program. A preferred method for evaluating the performance or quality of a program or product is to examine reviews posted on a reputable platform, such as the Warrior Forum.

Review Testimonials Carefully

Now that you have amassed a considerable collection of testimonials, we kindly request that you peruse and meticulously evaluate them. Naturally, do not anticipate a complete endorsement. Occasional negative reviews should not deter you from considering this product/service. Occasionally, individuals make the unfortunate decision of selecting an inappropriate product and subsequently express dissatisfaction with their choice. Endeavor to strike a balance between the positive and negative aspects. If the quantity of positive reviews significantly surpasses the negative ones, you can confidently determine the authenticity of the product or program in question.

There is a plethora of affiliate marketing ideas and tips available on the Internet. However, individuals fail to receive prior notification regarding the potential risks presented by deceptive individuals claiming to be 'affiliate marketing experts.' Individuals may attempt to entice you with offerings such as 'complimentary affiliate marketing reports' and 'remarkable super affiliate marketing techniques'. However, it is incumbent upon you to thoroughly assess each internet opportunity in terms of its past achievements, level of reliability, and rate of success.

Instructions On Utilizing Your Hoplink

This chapter aims to provide an in-depth understanding of the utilization of your Clickbank Hoplink.

Initially, let us gain a comprehensive understanding of the fundamentals of hoplink.

What Is a Hoplink?

A Hoplink is a URL designed for utilization as a referral tracking mechanism. At first glance, these URLs may resemble ordinary web addresses, but in reality, they possess distinctive properties. This is because a hoplink routes traffic to Clickbank's referral tracking system. Every individual hyperlink comprises personalized information that directs the individual clicking on the link to the vendor's website, with the intention of facilitating their purchase of the vendor's product.

The tracking system possesses the capability to ascertain the precise affiliate marketer responsible for referring the customer. If a patron selects a hyperlink that contains your hoplink and proceeds to make a purchase within a span of 60 days, you shall receive due credit for the transaction and duly obtain your commission.

Guide to Generating High-Quality Backlinks

An affiliate marketer has two options for generating a hoplink. The initial approach involves the automated generation of the hoplink through Clickbank's marketplace. You peruse the available merchandise and select the one you wish to endorse before proceeding to click on the 'Promote' button.

Subsequent to that, an automatically generated hypertext link will be provided to you, which has been specifically generated for your convenience. Simply copy the hyperlink URL and proceed to paste it in the location where you are promoting the product.

Another method for generating a hoplink involves utilizing your Clickbank account alias in conjunction with the alias of the product vendor you wish to endorse. This implies that it is necessary to be acquainted with both aliases in order to achieve success.

After obtaining your hoplink, it is essential to conduct a thorough assessment in order to verify its functionality. Kindly copy and paste the link onto your browser and verify if it redirects you to the vendor's webpage. If such an event occurs, kindly proceed by clicking the 'order now' button and direct your attention to the bottom section of the order form, where your nickname should be visible. Clickbank provides an additional encryption tool that enables users to enhance the security of their hoplink address.

How to Embed a Hoplink on a Web Page or Blog

Clickbank offers a convenient opportunity for bloggers and webmasters to generate income as affiliates by endorsing and advertising various digital products available within its marketplace.
If you possess a personal website or blog, you can leverage this opportunity to generate supplementary revenue by assuming the role of an affiliate marketer. By using your online platform to

endorse the products you have carefully selected to offer, you can tap into potential sources of income.

You can achieve this by strategically integrating hoplinks within your website or blog, allowing visitors to seamlessly navigate to the vendor's start page with the intention of enticing them to make a purchase. As a result, you will have the opportunity to earn commission-based income.

Register an account on Clickbank. Please proceed to log in and navigate the marketplace, where you will find an extensive array of digital products. Thoroughly examine the available options and select those that align with the specific niche of your blog or website.

This implies that you should seek out products that are compatible with your website or blog. For instance, if you engage in blogging about the latest applications for mobile phones, an electronic book providing guidance on app design could be considered a suitable choice.

Within the specific product you have selected, there exists a feature labeled as 'generate hoplink.' Kindly enter your account nickname in the designated field and proceed by selecting the 'create hoplink' button. Please copy and paste the hyperlink onto a notepad or any other word processing software and securely save it onto your personal computer. Please navigate to your blog and access the administration panel by logging in. Please proceed to select the option that will enable you to generate a post and compose a fresh entry relevant to your chosen product. Ensure that a pertinent location is selected to incorporate your hyperlink.

Emphasize the specific text that you wish to transform into a hyperlink, then select the option 'insert link' from the panel provided on your blog. Please retrieve and then insert the URL that you have previously saved on your computer into the designated link field. Please select the "save" option in order to preserve the hyperlink. Subsequently, proceed to post or publish your blog entry. Your blog currently incorporates your hoplink within the selected word or text.

If you are a webmaster, access the HTML editor and locate the desired text that you wish to transform into a hyperlink.

Embed the HTML code by hyperlinking the desired text or word to the specified location.

Please locate the hyperlink that you have stored on your computer and emphasize the 'URL' within the HTML code.

Substitute that element with the hoplink. Please substitute the current 'link text' with the text you have selected to convert into a hyperlink, and proceed to save the alterations.

How to Embed a Hyperlink into an Article

In the event that you do not possess a website or a blog, it remains possible to establish yourself as a proficient Clickbank affiliate marketer by producing well-crafted articles and subsequently distributing them to reputable article directories.

Compose an article utilizing any word processing software integrated into your personal computer. Kindly compose articles containing a minimum of 400 words, as the majority of article directories have a policy against accepting articles of shorter length.

Please ensure that you produce a high-quality article pertaining to a topic that is relevant to the product you are promoting.

Establish an account or enroll with any preferred article directory of your selection. After creating an account, proceed to sign in and select the option to compose an article.

Kindly transfer the article you have previously stored on your computer to the designated field specified by the article directory for submission.

Please proceed to the author biography section and compose a brief description of yourself or prepare a concise sales presentation for your product. Please select the desired text to utilize and convert into a hoplink.

Please locate the hyperlink that has been saved on your computer and paste it onto the selected text or word.

Kindly submit or publish your article. The article has now been updated with the addition of your hyperlink.

Please feel free to produce multiple articles to your satisfaction, ensuring that each article is original and unique. You have the option to submit them either to the same directory or distribute them across different directories.

Strategies for Identifying and Promoting Affiliate Products

Alright, I believe we have entertained ample conjecture for the present moment. Now, could you kindly elucidate the precise methodology underlying the establishment of your business and the initiation of your career as an affiliate marketer?

Initially, it is imperative that you obtain a suitable product. To acquire this, you will need to visit a website such as Clickbank or Commission Junction. JVZoo presents itself as a commendable alternative.

Here, you will have the opportunity to explore an extensive assortment of diverse products, all of which are integrated within affiliate networks. Kindly peruse the available choices and explore them at your leisure until you come across something that captivates your interest. You will come across relevant information pertaining to the assortment of products that are accessible for review. Therefore, it would be prudent of you to actively seek out this information. Products that are being sold at a reputable price point and offer a favorable commission are the ones on which you should concentrate your selling efforts.

Certain websites provide an opportunity to obtain a sales estimate, in which case it is advisable to seek out the products that are demonstrating notable success in the market.

Once you have determined the product that you intend to promote, the subsequent course of action entails establishing communication with the proprietor of the said product. If your endeavor proves fruitful, they will furnish you with a hyperlink, granting you the autonomy to employ it in any manner you deem appropriate.

Nevertheless, it is important to consider in this particular context that the vast majority of the merchandise provided by affiliates is bundled with accompanying promotional resources.

Maintain a constant awareness that your success is an indication of the creator's triumph as well. They are highly motivated to ensure your success, thus frequently providing you with resources like emails, a sales page, banner advertisements, and various marketing tools in numerous circumstances.

For individuals lacking prior experience in the marketing industry, I wholeheartedly recommend opting for a product that encompasses these supplementary benefits within its purchase package. By following this approach, you can promptly initiate operations by simply duplicating and inserting the materials accessible to you. Considering the identical nature of the product and the utilization of an identical marketing strategy, it is expected that you will observe a similar level of sales as previously experienced. Hence, there exists no justification for its failure to perform at the same level of efficacy as it demonstrated previously.

To reemphasize my previous statement, this framework represents a "replicate and duplicate" approach to managing a business. Another individual has already achieved successful sales of the product using a well-established approach, thus your actions merely involve replicating this technique to ensure that the funds will be transferred into your designated bank account.

Commercial Transactions Pertaining to Diverse Commodities and Services

Whilst utilizing a platform like JVZoo for the sale of eBooks presents a commendable strategy for maximizing profit margins, it is pertinent to acknowledge that this avenue also entails a set of disadvantages. Contrary to the assertions made by certain online marketers, it remains factual that physical goods continue to reign as the most sought-after products for sale on the internet.

Upon careful consideration, one will discern the inherent logic behind this proposition. What proportion of individuals within your circle of acquaintances engage in the acquisition of physical commodities? It is highly probable that such a statement applies to almost everyone. Nevertheless, how many individuals have you encountered who demonstrate a keen interest in acquiring an electronic book? Due to her inability to access PDF files, there is a potential limitation for your grandmother to read the book, unless she resorts to utilizing a Kindle device. Furthermore, given that your acquaintance lacks an affinity for reading, it is plausible that you too will not derive enjoyment from it.

Andasaresult,theportionofthemarketthat youcontrolwillbesignificantly reduced.

Therefore, the query at hand pertains to the approach that individuals engaged in affiliate marketing must adopt in order to effectively promote tangible merchandise. Opting to work as an Amazon Associate indisputably represents the predominant selection.

The associate scheme implemented by Amazon is the company's iteration of an affiliate program, which captivates numerous marketers with its enticing opportunities for participation.

Upon conducting a search on affiliate marketing, it is likely that a significant majority of the available resources will primarily emphasize the promotion and sale of digital products via renowned platforms such as JVZoo, ClickBank, and Commission Junction. This is due to the fact that these platforms facilitate the seamless monitoring of sales and inventory management.

On Amazon, operations are conducted in a distinct manner. Amazon presently disseminates the proceeds with the manufacturer. Moreover, Amazon incurs expenses for warehousing, shipping, and postage. Consequently, Amazon typically extends an offer of not more than 4% of the profits, with the potential for increasing it to 8% if negotiated assertively.

This suggests that in order to attain profitability, it will be necessary to sell a substantial quantity of additional items at considerably higher prices.

Nevertheless, does this insinuate that one should abstain from contemplating the utilization of Amazon Associates? Absolutely not.

To commence, the trade of tangible goods generally yields a substantially superior level of profitability compared to the trade of digital products. Consider the following: are you inclined to allocate a substantial amount of funds towards an item that you can physically possess and proudly exhibit to your acquaintances, or are you more inclined to allocate a significant amount of funds towards a digital experience that necessitates reading on a computer screen?

Furthermore, Amazon is widely recognized as a distinguished and reliable corporation that garners the trust and confidence of consumers. This suggests a heightened inclination for them to make a purchase from the aforementioned entity, with the added convenience of completing the transaction through a single click.

Due to Amazon's extensive inventory, one can rest assured that there will be a suitable companion for nearly every item to be sold.

Lastly, in the event that a customer selects your URL and subsequently makes a different purchase on Amazon, you will still receive remuneration for the initial click. If, for instance, an individual were to purchase a new computer, and you were to receive a commission of 8% from that transaction, it has the capacity to generate a notable increment of supplementary earnings. Provided that the customer was initially referred to Amazon by you, irrespective of any direct promotional efforts on your part, you would still qualify for the commission.

What course of action would you suggest for me? Employ the utilization of both strategies in affiliate marketing. However, it is essential to duly incorporate Amazon in your analysis as a failure to do so would result in an incomplete assessment.

In the forthcoming chapters, you will acquire knowledge about effectively marketing Amazon products in a distinctive manner, enabling you to optimize the potential benefits offered by these products.

(Please take into consideration: A limitation imposed by the Amazon Associates program stipulates that individuals residing in a different country than Amazon are ineligible to receive financial remuneration.) In alternative terms, if you possess a business within the confines of the United Kingdom, it will be necessary for you to guide your clientele towards the British iteration of Amazon's online platform. You are still permitted to generate sales on Amazon.com, however, the resulting proceeds may only be acquired in the form of vouchers.

Alternative Approaches to Marketing and Selling Tangible Goods

In regards to the transaction of physical goods, it is evident that Amazon is not the sole feasible choice. There exists a vast multitude of authentic retailers in the market, with an even greater number of manufacturers engaging in direct collaborations with marketers to offer affiliate programs.

You may discover that by diligently exploring alternative options, you can identify a subject that is significantly more closely aligned with the focal point of your website. This is a piece of information that can be unveiled by conducting thorough research on alternative products, thereby increasing the probability of successful sales.

When initiating a search on Google for these affiliate programs, one can simply input the designation of their market segment, followed by the phrase 'affiliate program.' Moreover, the online realm bestows an abundance of resources in the shape of rankings that evaluate the most prosperous affiliate programs in each specific domain.

You also have the option to redirect customers to a manufacturer or vendor that does not currently offer an affiliate program... and subsequently inquire with them regarding the feasibility of establishing one for your specific needs. If you can successfully accomplish this, you will have the opportunity to secure an exclusive agreement and potentially earn a significant commission.

Evidently, it is imperative that you demonstrate the extent of your reach and influence in order to establish the rationale for their collaboration with you.

Facilitating the Sale of Services

In addition, one may consider the option of promoting a service or offering an SAS (Software As a Service) for sale. This course of action presents the opportunity for generating the greatest financial gain.

This is attributable to the significant availability of services that offer recurring commissions. Suppose you achieve success in persuading an individual to register an account on a gambling platform. Certain online gambling platforms offer a provision where they incentivize continued patronage by offering a percentage-based remuneration on the ongoing profits generated by a player, as long as the player maintains their status as a customer of the website.

If you are able to convince an individual to enroll in a hosting account or join a recurring service, you will often be presented with a recurring commission that will be disbursed to you on a monthly basis as long as they continue their affiliation with the hosting company. Similarly, should you succeed in convincing someone to subscribe to a recurring service, you will discover that a commission is extended to you as well.

As a matter of course, initially, this may entail a rather inconsequential sum of commission. Nevertheless, this may lead to a substantial extension of the overall duration. In the coming years, it is possible that your website could experience a significant increase in conversions, potentially reaching into the hundreds or even thousands. These conversions would subsequently result in recurring financial gains for you, even in the event of your site's closure. In the event that this occurs, you stand to gain without incurring any losses.

Strategies for Selecting a Specific Market Segment

Welcome to part two. In the ensuing segment, we shall deliberate upon the paramount importance of carefully choosing the appropriate niche for one's blog. This is of fundamental importance for your success, as a failure to select the appropriate field may result in unfavorable consequences. Should you happen to choose an inappropriate niche for your blog, it would be necessary for you to relinquish any aspirations of becoming a full-time blogger.

When it comes to selecting the appropriate niche for your blog, there are several factors to consider prior to finalizing the appropriate topic. It is advisable to carefully ascertain that the topic you intend to compose on is not excessively saturated, indicating the absence of a substantial number of bloggers who have already written extensively about it.

Surprisingly, there is no requirement for a highly specialized theme, suggesting that it may pose challenges in guiding users to the website. In summary, it would be advantageous to ensure the presence of excellent affiliate options for the specific niche. Although most specialties offer alternative options, it is worth pondering whether these choices will yield a financial benefit.

In this section, we will illustrate the highly sought-after strategies for identifying a niche that not only aligns with your expertise, but is unique to your individual skillset. Furthermore, I will provide you with several strategies for identifying a suitable topic to write about that already garners an optimal level of traffic, enabling you to commence earning a monetary income. Immediately, why don't we delve into the rudimentary aspects of this component.

Select a specialized area of interest that appeals to you

If you are not serious in your approach to the subject matter being discussed, it is highly unlikely that you will generate any financial gains from it. Individuals possess a remarkable ability to discern individuals who are not engaged with the subject matter. It is imperative that you select a specialty for your blog with the utmost care, ensuring that it aligns with your genuine interest or at least a moderate level of curiosity.

The most optimal method for discovering your niche is to introspect and identify your personal interests and hobbies. If I happen to have a strong affinity for yoga and regularly engage in yoga practices, then it may be a prospective avenue for you. Take a moment to ponder upon your hobbies or areas of personal interest. Each individual possesses a particular passion or pastime that brings them joy. I am highly confident that you also possess the aforementioned capability, therefore I encourage you to explore and express it.

Boutique-sized specialization.

Once you have chosen a topic to write about, it is now appropriate to familiarize yourself with the competition. To ascertain, navigate to your area of expertise on Google and locate the "About" section directly below the search engine.

You will observe a numerical quantity that is potentially in the range of several millions. In order to select the appropriate specialty, it is advisable to consider a numerical range below 50 million or exceeding 1 million. This range can be considered the optimal threshold for prioritizing your decision. Any amount exceeding 50 million would result in a significant level of involvement, while any amount below 1 million would indicate a lower likelihood of achieving profitability.

Affiliate marketing

In subsequent sections, we will delve deeper into the exploration of partner promotion. It is imperative that you engage in thorough research and ascertain your prospects in your chosen field prior to commencing your blog. For readers who are unfamiliar with the concept of affiliate marketing, it involves featuring a product on your blog and providing a link that is solely relevant to your website. Whenever an individual opts to make a purchase of that specific product through your referral link, you shall receive a monetary commission.

Affiliate marketing serves as the primary source of income for the majority, if not all, of bloggers, thus it is crucial not to overlook this aspect. The most optimal method to ascertain if your subject possesses the appropriate affiliate program entails visiting Amazon.com and examining all the merchandise available for purchase pertaining to your specific niche. If a substantial assortment of merchandise is available for your promotion, then you have identified the suitable option. In a subsequent section, we will discuss further alternatives pertaining to partner promotion. However, for the present moment, it is imperative to focus on Amazon and the range of products they offer.

Monetizing

By implementing a monetization strategy for your blog site, you are essentially granting permission to

Google to display advertisements on your platform. Every time users click on that advertisement, you will definitely generate income. The most effective approach to ascertain the level of Google advertising for your specific niche is to conduct a search using your designated "keyword."

Should your topic pertain to yoga exercise, kindly input "yoga exercise" into the search field within the Google search engine. The greater the exposure you have to targeted advertisements within your specific niche, the increased potential you possess for monetizing your blog effectively. Earning revenue from is an exemplary strategy to generate additional income from your blog, particularly if your blog attracts a substantial number of visitors.

Final research

Presently, in order to ensure the acquisition of a firm grasp on your subject matter, it is imperative to access the platform known as "Google Trends." Within this forum, you will be able to ascertain the level of popularity and active pursuit of articles pertaining to your specific niche. You simply have to input your search query into the search engine, and it will generate a graphical representation for you.

Please ensure that you are taking into consideration a chart containing a minimum of five years' worth of data. If your representation consistently maintains a prominent and unwavering position, then you have indeed chosen the appropriate subject. In the event that there is a consistent downward trend in your chart over the years, it would be opportune for you to explore a fresh topic for your blog.

If all these criteria are taken into consideration, then you will have identified the suitable niche and can promptly commence your blog. If that is not the case, then I kindly request you to reevaluate your topics and consider selecting a new one that fully satisfies all of the criteria detailed above.

However, it is imperative to ensure that you are generating revenue from your blog rather than purely writing on it.

Continue exploring and persevering, and you will ultimately discover your valuable subject. Rest assured, it is imperative that you possess the capability to identify your subject amidst a variety of frames.

The Blueprint For Establishing A Lucrative Advertising Agency Worth Millions

In the forthcoming chapter, you will be introduced to a comprehensive guide detailing the sequential process of initiating a highly lucrative marketing enterprise that yields six-digit revenue, thereby allowing you to commence receiving commission immediately, possibly as early as this evening. One advantageous aspect of engaging in online affiliate marketing resides in the ability to build a business centered upon one's personal interests and zeal. It is not constrained by a specific geographic location and affords individuals the liberty to earn income while traversing the globe.

I intend to divulge to you the methods through which you can expand your marketing enterprise, potentially achieving a revenue of 1.5 million dollars within a span of 5 months, all without relying on an existing audience, products, clients, personnel, or technical expertise. The formula I am presenting to you has been substantiated. It is utilized by both the most modest and the most prominent digital marketers globally. It necessitates minimal exertion and possesses the capacity to grant you the opportunity for a four-hour work week.

I would like to provide further elucidation on the matter, emphasizing that this is not a scheme or gimmick designed to facilitate rapid wealth accumulation, nor does it involve any loopholes or tricks that may lead to unfavorable consequences. Promote active engagement and cultivate a diligent attitude. No online endeavor achieves success without a deliberate commitment to exert effort. An advantageous aspect of this formula is that it does not necessitate a substantial amount of capital as a starting point, enabling individuals to lead a life commensurate with their rightful entitlements.

To achieve the level of success enjoyed by the world's leading affiliates, one must possess just three essential elements in order for their marketing business to generate a six-figure income. It is necessary to have individuals, location, and merchandise. One effective approach to reach individuals is by employing Facebook advertisements, which can successfully capture their interest and drive their engagement. Your presell page serves as the designated platform for the sale of goods and services to customers. The objective of this page is to address a issue individuals encounter in their lives. Direct their attention towards achieving your intended audience transition from a social mentality to a consumer mindset in order to enhance your conversion rates and maximize your profits.

The product will serve as your affiliated offering to your targeted clientele. The optimal promotions within this framework ought to attract substantial, extensive, and untargeted visitor demographics. One effective method to encourage individuals to convert is by utilizing an advertisement featuring a video rather than a still image. If an image conveys a thousand words, then an image will undoubtedly communicate a million. A convenient method for locating videos to incorporate into your advertisements is to explore websites such as Pond5. What is the increased probability of capturing attention and garnering a higher number of clicks on an advertisement when employing a video that elucidates your concerns, as opposed to utilizing an image? Videos typically demonstrate superior effectiveness compared to still images.

In relation to your presell page, it is advised to adhere to a predetermined script and prioritize proven strategies rather than attempting to create your own sales presentation. Affiliate marketers possess a keen intellect in crafting persuasive presell page pitches. They subject these sales to testing and optimization to maximize their conversion rates before delivering them to you. You stand to generate greater financial returns by adhering to the preexisting information that has been made accessible to you.

It is not advisable to engage in the creation of your own presell pages due to the considerable amount of time, creative effort, technical expertise required, and the potential downside of low clickthrough rates despite the considerable investment involved. Another suggestion within this formula is to exclusively endorse products or offers that have significant demand and are being purchased extensively. Refrain from seeking out products that may sound appealing. In the realm of affiliate marketing, it is discouraged to show support for the less favored.

Technical skills tend to be unfavorable due to their potential to impede efficiency, the challenges associated with learning them, the potential for errors, the subsequent time required for rectification, and the availability of tools that automate tasks instead of relying solely on manual efforts.

A prevalent error that is revealed by this formula is the failure to utilize swipe files. Certain affiliate marketers choose not to utilize this strategy, and you are already at an advantage because you are demonstrating the foresight to incorporate this valuable resource. A swipe file, in essence, comprises a compilation of well-established and validated advertising materials. I highly recommend employing a swipe file as it greatly facilitates the process of launching advertisements. These files consist of an array of interchangeable headlines and images that can be judiciously combined to identify a triumphant combination. Moreover, utilizing a swipe file will help you economize your valuable time that would otherwise be expended on extensive research to identify the most effective images and headlines.

In regards to affiliate marketing, what are your thoughts on which option would yield greater profitability? I will present a scenario to you and kindly request your endeavor to provide the most suitable response based on your capabilities. Assume that there exist two separate islands populated by a sizable number of individuals. On one island, there reside individuals lacking footwear, while on the other island, there reside individuals possessing footwear. In your informed opinion, which island do you believe would provide favorable prospects for promoting shoes?

The most suitable island for shoe promotion would consist of individuals who are already in possession of footwear. The rationale behind this is that individuals on the island who are observed wearing shoes have been reliably identified as purchasers. There might be several factors present on the island that could dissuade them from buying any shoes. It could potentially be an uninhabited landmass characterized by an expanse of sandy terrain, rendering footwear unnecessary. An additional factor might be the prohibitively high cost associated with transporting footwear to that particular island.

To achieve success in the field of affiliate marketing, one must adhere to strategies that have proven effective in the market. You should consistently focus on individuals who possess purchasing propensity. The approach employed by individuals when directing their advertisements is typically based on targeting various elements such as interests, categories, and age demographics. The issue at hand is that these affiliate marketers are conducting their business based on conjecture. Relying on speculation will not afford you the opportunity to establish a viable and enduring enterprise.

The formula I am elucidating to you is a precise approach to Facebook advertising that eliminates conjecture, employing a method of targeting known as the 1-5-10 approach. This entails the act of uploading a roster of individuals who have previously made a purchase via Facebook. Facebook's course of action will involve utilizing the aforementioned file, containing the email address of the buyer, to cross-reference individuals who display similar potential for purchasing the product.

Facebook will thoroughly examine all additional distinguishing features and correlations, thus generating what is commonly referred to as a "lookalike audience" of purchasers. This implies that you are provided with the utmost efficacious advertising tools. One advantage of using this formula is that it allows for efficient utilization of cutting-edge artificial intelligence algorithms to precisely target your advertisements.

The formula that I am presenting to you has the capability to facilitate your sales across multiple diverse niches and marketplaces. The advantage of possessing this formula lies in obtaining a seed list (a compilation of buyers) for a range of programs. The formula I am elucidating for you is the Super Affiliate System developed by John Crestani. He provides a comprehensive strategy pertaining to paid advertising that enables individuals to generate substantial earnings online while effectively targeting various market segments. Presented herein are the three cardinal tenets highlighting the quintessence of generating substantial online commissions.

Secret #1: Effective presell pages serve as a significant strategic advantage for highly successful affiliates.

Secret #2: The process of crafting video advertisements is straightforward and yields significantly superior results compared to static images.

Secret #3: Possessing buyer data is essential for effective targeting.

Outlined below are several notable benefits associated with the utilization of The Super Affiliate System.

First advantage: The system can be set up without the need for any programming.

Advantage #2: Exceptional conversion rates maximized by highly appealing offers.

One benefit is the implementation of effective advertisements that generate strong engagement.

Advantage #4: Presell pages with a high conversion rate

Advantage #5: Acquiring comprehensive buyer data for precision targeting with minimal uncertainty.

In order to generate substantial wealth through this established approach, there are three prerequisites to adhere to.

Condition #1: It is imperative to adhere to ethical principles while utilizing the system.

Requirement #2: You must exhibit a willingness to listen attentively, acquire knowledge, and effectively implement the prescribed system.

The comprehensive affiliate training program provides instruction on a straightforward five-minute technique that yields $460 commissions by leveraging a complimentary source of traffic. How to utilize social media platforms to generate a steady stream of online revenue. The present discourse unveils a lesser-known advertising technique on Facebook that one can employ for effectively reaching individuals interested in making purchases, regardless of the absence of a list of potential buyers. In addition, there is a straightforward 30-minute activity that will stimulate your mind to instinctively pursue achievement, regardless of any previous lack of success in your previous entrepreneurial endeavors or limited experience in the realm of online affiliate marketing.

It encompasses an supplementary video-based instructional program that is designed to facilitate the rapid generation of substantial commissions within a condensed timeframe.

Week 1: Introduction to the model.

Week 2: Establishing your virtual sales representative

Week 3: Developing your monetized advertisement

Week 4: Engaging in comprehensive preparations for optimal achievement.

Week 5: Achieve a daily revenue of $460 under your control.

Week 6: Expanding Your Business

By enrolling below, you will gain access to these exclusive advantages, elevating your affiliate marketing to a higher caliber.

Included in the package is a comprehensive collection of affiliate marketing training videos, spanning a total duration of 15 hours, meticulously crafted by esteemed affiliate marketing expert, John Crestani.

Prepared for the commencement of affiliate campaigns, providing you with essential buyer data for precise targeting, verified ads that can be duplicated effortlessly, established presell pages that can be seamlessly utilized, and high-performing products to effectively sell on the internet.

Utilize user-friendly ad swipes: Gain access to a collection of established and highly engaging advertisements for effortless drag-and-drop use.

Establishing network referrals leading to prominent affiliate networks hosting highly lucrative offers.

• Being granted with the opportunity to attend John Crestani's live webinars on a weekly basis, wherein you will have the chance to seek clarification on any inquiries you may possess and receive individualized guidance pertaining to your current advancements.

In conclusion, you will be granted access to a comprehensive training and technology system of unmatched quality, which encompasses a genuine value exceeding $37,223.

The comprehensive marketing course, curated by esteemed instructor John Crestani, features 15 hours of invaluable content, equating to a substantial value of $10,000.

Buyer data: Transfer and insert information for the purpose of advertisement targeting (valued at $12,000)

Proven advertisement templates available: Easily import and utilize highly effective ads with drag and drop functionality (valued at $2,000)

Preselling page templates: Easily duplicate and customize without the need for programming skills (Equivalent to a $4,000 value)

Access to the community is priced at $747.

Participation in the exclusive weekly live training sessions led by John Crestani, a highly esteemed expert in the field ($7976 estimated value)

The collective value of these resources amounts to $37,223. Should you decide to embark on the transformative journey of achieving personal growth and living the life that aligns with your true potential, the exclusive offer can be availed at a nominal price of $997 through the provided hyperlink.

Methods For Identifying Products To Promote

The absence of a product results in the absence of a market. Having a product is indispensable for being regarded as a marketer. Therefore, the task of identifying products for market promotion is a crucial undertaking that will ultimately ascertain the extent of your achievements in the field of affiliate marketing.

Factors to consider in selecting your niche product

The subsequent set of standards will assist you in determining the optimal product niche.

Select a specific product category that corresponds to your core interests - Blogging revolves around one's ardor and enthusiasm. Hence, it is imperative to select a product niche that is consistent with your fervor in order to harmonize it with your content. In the role of an affiliate marketer, you function as a publisher. Attempting to disseminate content that lacks alignment with your passion will inevitably result in premature exhaustion. Unyielding ardor is the impetus behind your perseverance in writing, even in the face of adversity. Affiliate marketing should be viewed as a long-term commitment rather than a short-term endeavor. The emphasis lies on achieving long-term benefits rather than immediate profits. Numerous individuals prematurely surrender due to their disillusionment with the product's lack of immediate success in the market. This would not hold true if you were blogging out of passion, as any income earned would merely be an additional perk.

Select a product niche that is accessible on your preferred network platform. It's important to note that not all network platforms are identical in terms of offerings. There are establishments that possess reputation and are compatible with your requirements, and there are establishments that do not fulfill those criteria. Once you have made a determination regarding the optimal platform, evaluate the assortment of products available and ascertain whether your product niche aligns with them. In the event that it does not, it would be advisable to identify an alternative option that closely aligns with your preferred platform or product niche.

Select a product of considerable profitability – The profitability of a product can be evaluated based on several factors, including the commission structure (both in terms of rate and amount), the anticipated turnover rate (i.e., frequency of sales within a specific period, such as a month), and the desired minimum rate of return on investment (e.g., expenses related to hosting and publication). Various product vendors have varying rates of commission. However, various network platforms provide varying rates of commission for the identical product. Therefore, as you determine the most lucrative product, conduct thorough research to determine the optimum commission rate across the leading platforms.

Select a product that is suitable for sustained marketing efforts over an extended period. Seasonal and limited-time offerings may not be optimal for your affiliate marketing endeavors, especially if you are in the early stages of establishing your presence, as they may dwindle in popularity over time. If you desire your affiliate marketing enterprise to yield returns, opt for products that will sustain a steady demand for the foreseeable future. By doing so, you have the ability to produce enduring content, referred to as evergreen content, which maintains its relevance for an extensive duration. As long as the product remains available and your affiliate link remains active, you will continue to generate earnings through ongoing promotion of your affiliate links associated with this content.

The Comprehensive Guide to Affiliate Marketing

It would be beneficial for you to have a comprehensive understanding of the commonly used terminology in affiliate marketing. Indeed, even the most comprehensive educational programs may fail to fully elucidate the intricacies of various terms (if at all). Presented below is a comprehensive compendium encompassing commonly employed terminologies in the realm of affiliate marketing, arranged in alphabetical order from A to Z:

A hindrance to progress in terms of promotion

A promotion deterrent is a software code that users activate within their applications to prevent advertisements from being displayed on websites. The prevalence of ad blockers has significantly increased over time, with an estimated 15% of Internet users employing some form of ad blocking software. Promotion obstacles present detrimental information for associates in advertising. In the eventuality that your promotion fails to materialize, you will not accrue any commissions. Regrettably, a plethora of unscrupulous advertisers has given rise to the development of this technology. Currently, there exist no viable alternatives to employing adblocking technology.

Alteration in exchange rate

This is another crucial measurement. Utilizing our click-through rate model mentioned earlier, you direct a total of 500 individuals to the member offer that you are promoting. The quantity of individuals who engage in a purchase is employed to calculate your conversion rate.

Thus, if 50 individuals out of the 500 were to make a purchase, your conversion rate would be 10%. In a similar fashion to the navigation rates, increasing your conversion rates will yield superior results. Members may evaluate conversion rates for different promotions. They can employ paid traffic to gain discernment into the quantity of their clicks that result in sales. If the exchange rate is high, they have the opportunity to invest in additional traffic in order to generate increased revenue.

⬛ Unit Cost

Under the methodology of cost per activity (CPA) promotion, affiliates are eligible to receive a commission if a visitor, who accesses their affiliate link, successfully completes a specific action. This may entail tasks such as inputting their email address, completing a simple form, providing their postal code, and so on.

Many auxiliary advertisers prefer to incorporate CPA offers, as they do not require a sale for commission to be earned. The conversion rates associated with CPA offers generally tend to be significantly higher as there is no requirement for the guest to make a purchase. Nevertheless, it is not uncommon for commission rates associated with CPA offers to be comparatively lower than those for transactional arrangements.

Cost per transaction" or "expense per transaction

The cost per deal (CPD) is widely recognized as the most prominent form of partner offers. The subordinate receives a mutually agreed-upon commission for each instance in which a customer referred by them completes a purchase. In general, it can be observed that CPS offers tend to boast higher commission rates compared to CPA or CPL offers. However, this is not typically the case, thus it is crucial to conduct thorough research.

"⬚ Lead Acquisition Cost (LAC)

Cost per lead (CPL) promotion is typically where a guest needs to give their email address, call a particular telephone number, or give another way to the sponsor to reach them. A member advertiser can receive a commission with CPL offers without the necessity of any transaction taking place.

Subsequent Associations

The subsequent affiliation will provide insight into the sources from which your guests originate. You may be utilizing certain traffic hotspots for your affiliate campaigns and you are interested in determining which one is yielding the most favorable outcomes. Certain affiliated organizations will provide you with the following contacts which you may utilize for this purpose. Numerous esteemed advertisers prefer to employ external tracking services such as Snap Enchantment as they offer a wealth of additional information.

Introduction page

A welcome page is a website page that you direct your visitors to upon clicking on your hyperlinks. This could pertain directly to the business page pertaining to the specific product or service, for instance. Astute partner advertisers have opted to redirect their visitors to dedicated landing pages instead of directly linking them to a sales page.

Arguably, the most compelling incentive to proceed with this action involves obtaining the email address of the guest.

Once you obtain their email address, you can subsequently redirect them to the seller's page containing exclusive offers. Additionally, you have the option to employ a landing page or a gateway page to preheat your visitor prior to their arrival at the seller's sales page.

Certain advertising agencies have restrictions in place regarding the direct redirection of visitors to a sales-oriented webpage. Google and Facebook will require you to create an informative landing page. The subsequent destination for the guest will be determined by your discretion.

Perceptions

Impressions refer to the instances when your promotional or auxiliary message is displayed. Several websites implement a billing strategy known as "cost per thousand impressions (CPM)" where sponsors are required to pay. In the realm of email marketing, impressions occur when a recipient engages with your messages by opening them and viewing the attached affiliate advertisements.

⬚ Data Streams

Certain member organizations or projects may provide their subsidiaries with an information feed that can be utilized on their respective websites. The document consists of the products and services offered by a marketer, encompassing various items such as...

● Product or service titles.

● Expenses associated with the goods or services ● Expenditures for the items or services ● Charges for the products or services ● Outlays for the items or services ● Fees for the products or services

● Visual representations of the products or services

Instances of depiction

● Fascinating collaborative counterparts

A derivative can leverage this information stream to display the complete range of products on their website. In the event that the visitor clicks on the affiliate rat within the information feed to obtain additional details and subsequently completes a purchase, the affiliate shall receive a commission.

▢ Prospects" "▢ Potential customers" "▢ Prospective clientele

Should you possess any inclination to achieve success in the field of affiliate marketing, it is advisable to actively pursue both leads and potential business opportunities. Through the implementation of a welcome page that captures the email address of your visitor initially, you are establishing a valuable opportunity to engage with them on multiple occasions. A subset of the leads will utilize your affiliate code to make purchases, thereby resulting in additional commissions. "Email leads hold great importance as they enable you to establish prompt and ongoing communication with your visitors at your convenience."

In the event that you happen to refer a visitor solely to the vendor's sales page, there exists a risk of permanently losing them if they fail to make a purchase. Not all individuals will immediately make a purchase upon encountering a promotion. Collecting email leads enables you to engage in direct communication with your visitors once again.

⬛ Member Mission

A member campaign entails the promotion of a product or service to a specific target audience by you, the affiliate. Frequently the item or administration merchant will have a deals channel that you can advance. You will receive an agreed-upon commission from the merchant for each transaction you complete.

Member crusades revolve around effectively channeling targeted traffic towards an associate proposal. You have the option to select either a complimentary or premium partner campaign:

Unrestricted traffic derived from virtual entertainment, web search engines, and various alternative channels

Monetized traffic derived from digital entertainment advertisements or search engine advertisements

All esteemed member endeavors will promptly furnish comprehensive reports on their ability to generate traffic, convert leads into tangible business opportunities, provide detailed traffic sources analysis, and much more. After reviewing the metrics of your partner missions, you can subsequently implement modifications to enhance conversion rates, for instance.

⬜ Affiliated Entity

A partner network is a platform that provides users with access to a wide range of affiliated offers. Among the most widely acclaimed partner networks in existence is

Clickbank.com provides access to a plethora of diverse affiliate opportunities.

Subsidiary organizations typically provide substantial data regarding their affiliate offerings. One can typically ascertain the popularity and efficacy of a product or service by observing its conversion rate, potential commission earnings, and other relevant factors of appraisal.

Offshoot networks facilitate the convergence of product and service providers with merchants and partners. Unless a seller possesses a partner program, they will enlist the assistance of a member organization to inform affiliates about their promotions. Certain member organizations have implemented a systematic endorsement process to promote their products and services. It is expected that you obtain endorsement from individual vendors of the respective items.

⬜ Manage pricing structures

The Click-Through Rate (CTR) is a crucial metric that quantifies the number of times your affiliated advertisement is selected by users. The rate at which this information is communicated relies on the quantity of impressions that your connection receives. If you are able to achieve a high Click-Through Rate, then your chances of earning higher commissions will significantly increase.

Assuming that you possess an email database comprising 10,000 individuals who support your cause. You transmit an email containing your members report and experience a 5,000 readership among your supporters. This indicates that your connection has achieved a total of 5,000 impressions. If, by any chance, 500 of your subscribers were to click on your link, your click-through rate (CTR) would be 10%.

Request of standard value

This is where the affiliated organization will disclose the standard request value for each affiliate transaction. There are several products and services that offer upgrades, allowing customers to enhance their purchase. These offers pertain to the "back end" and will be presented to the client following their purchase of the initial front end item or service.

The standard inquiry value shall take into account these proposed modifications. You will observe the customary quantum of fiscal transactions made by customers upon purchasing a particular product. This is of great importance, as typically, you will receive commissions on both upgrades and initial sales.

Part Evaluation

Experimental analysis, often referred to as A/B testing, involves evaluating the performance of multiple advertisements promoting the same affiliate offer. You have the opportunity to conduct split tests utilizing paid traffic arrangements offered by notable suppliers such as Google, YouTube, and other recognized entities. Employ the diverse metrics provided to assess which marketing campaign is yielding the most favorable results.

🔲 Levels of engagement with partners

A subsidiary exposure refers to a statement provided on your website that clarifies your partnership role in promoting and endorsing certain products and services. At this juncture, it is imperative to inform your website visitors that in the event they utilize the hyperlinks provided on your website leading to purchases, you may receive compensation in the form of a commission.

The United States Government Exchange Commission has enacted a regulation mandating that all affiliate advertisers include a subsidiary disclosure on their website. Failure to accomplish this can result in substantial monetary penalties.

⯀ Offer Extended to Partners

A derivative offer refers to a distinctive product or service that can be promoted in exchange for a commission payment. The majority of member organizations will provide comprehensive information on the available offshoot offers, including significant metrics such as sales volume, conversion rates, and more.

For every subsidiary proposition, there will typically be an exclusive member link made accessible. When a visitor clicks on this link, they will be redirected to the product or service sales funnel, and you will receive appropriate credit for the transaction. In the event that they happen to make any purchases, you will earn commissions.

⦿ Collaborative Alliance Initiative

A subsidiary program is a structural framework that enables product and service vendors to engage affiliates by offering a means to register and provide commission payments. The merchant has the ability to determine the percentage of commission they will allocate for each transaction. Branches will leverage the program to enroll as a subsidiary and to procure their unique affiliate partners.

Remuneration based on the number of photographs taken

Guest traffic generated by search engine crawlers such as Google and Bing is commonly regarded as exceptional. This is due to the fact that customers employ a specific search term (keyword) in order to locate the desired information. In the capacity of a subsidiary, you have the option to procure PPC traffic from esteemed platforms such as Google or Microsoft, thereby effectively directing targeted visitors to your offerings.

The volume of PPC traffic was initially quite limited, but over the years, it has experienced a significant increase in cost. Typically, the cost of advertising on Microsoft platforms such as Bing and MSN is comparatively lower than that of Google PPC. It would be beneficial to perform the calculations in this context. Purchasing website traffic is an exceptional approach for conducting experiments on modifications for offers, as it allows for the acquisition of targeted visitors within a matter of minutes.

⊡ Net income per photo

This is an additional crucial measurement that you should keep in mind. All of the subordinate entities or initiatives may provide EPC statistics pertaining to their products and services. The Earnings Per Click (EPC) is conveyed in a monetary format, such as $10, and represents the proportion of the commission amount that an affiliate will earn for each click of their affiliate weasel.

• Gain from Speculation (financial return on investment) • Profitability derived from Speculation (yield on invested capital) • Returns generated through Speculation (financial earnings from investment) • Monetary gains resulting from Speculation (financial benefits from investment)

If you find yourself expending significant financial resources on your associate marketing endeavors, it is crucial to ascertain the returns gained from this investment. Deduct all mission expenses from the net income that you receive (your bonuses). This will provide you with prompt insights regarding the productivity and effectiveness of your missions. You are required to achieve the highest possible return on your initial capital investment.

Incentives

In the realm of affiliate marketing, the competition can be fiercely intense. However, by offering unique incentives to customers that other affiliates cannot provide, you will secure a distinct advantage. Rewards are frequently extended within the realm of online money-making or internet marketing.

For example, if you were to propose a supplementary proposal that demonstrates the process of creating an email list and marketing to it, you could provide your email templates as an additional incentive. These are previous communications that you have employed that have exhibited commendable conversion rates. If a customer perceives that you are providing the most advantageous incentives, they will make use of your partner connect to make their purchase, thereby earning you the commission.

The Procedure For Initiating The Process

Every prosperous endeavor commences with progression and subsequently strategizing. Use this introductory checklist to aid you in effectively getting organized and embarking on the path towards affiliate marketing success.

marketing profits.

1. Gain a comprehensive understanding of your target audience by conducting thorough research. Where is their preferred social gathering spot? What causes them sleepless nights. From whom do they prefer to receive information?

2. Identify the Concerns of Your Target Audience – Explore and understand at least three areas of concern that can be alleviated through your expertise and

the innovative solutions you have developed or come across.

3. Understand Your Purpose – It is imperative that you ascertain the underlying reasons for your concern towards this target audience and your qualifications as the most suitable individual to discover or develop the products that serve as solutions for them.

4. Develop a branded website specifically tailored to engage your target audience. Properly addressing your audience is crucial, as it ensures they immediately comprehend the essence and values of your brand.

5. Establishing Branded Social Platforms - Similarly, your social platforms should be correctly branded to ensure clear identification as your own.

6. Configure your email autoresponder - Establishing an effective email marketing strategy is paramount to your success. Begin building your subscriber list in advance of product availability, enticing potential subscribers through the utilization of giveaways, checklists, and enticing blog content.

7. Establish Your Funnels - Employ cutting-edge technology to streamline and automate your marketing funnels for each individual product you intend to endorse to your target audience.

8. Infuse your website and social media platforms with tailored content - Develop a comprehensive content marketing strategy that revolves around addressing the specific needs, concerns, and preferences of your audience for each product or service offered.

9. Select a Product for Promotion – Considering the preferences of your

target audience, identify premium products that align with your values and can be effectively endorsed through partnerships with reputable companies that prioritize superior customer service.

10. Embrace the role of an Affiliate for That Product – Enroll as an affiliate should you have the means to access the relevant information in order to communicate with them regarding it. Do not hesitate to persist even in the face of initial rejection; focus on personal growth and consider revisiting the opportunity as needed.

11. Develop Content Centered on the Product – Be mindful of crafting content that aligns with the products intended for promotion, tailored to suit each individual's purchasing stage.

journey.

12. Employ All-Around Content Promotion - Utilize technology to strategically promote your content across various platforms, even in instances where it is offered at no cost. Perhaps you should consider promoting it as your most expensive item.

13. Verify Your Figures - Consistently analyze your numerical data to ensure that your actions yield the desired outcomes.

14. Repeat – Don't stop. Maintain consistency and persevere in achieving the desired outcome. Revise considering your circumstances

metrics.

The primary inquiry at present pertains to what you are awaiting. Affiliate marketing proves to be a highly profitable endeavor

Commencing a profession, even in a part-time capacity. There is no need for you to accomplish all of it today. Start at

Initiate and oversee the cycle. Before you know it, the initial payment will commence to be deposited into your bank account.

Creating A Website

Certain individuals who are knowledgeable in the field of Internet marketing may inform you that it is possible to engage in affiliate advertising without the need for a website. That is genuine. However, the inclusion of your website will substantially simplify matters and greatly augment your profitability.

A website serves as a virtual workspace, akin to an office within the online realm. If legitimate enterprises possess physical retail locations, your affiliate marketing business will establish a website as its digital headquarters. The advantage of possessing your website primarily lies in its function as a platform intricately linked to your business operations, serving as an eminent hub where you can direct individuals, thereby exposing them to your business message.

As an affiliate marketer, you can leverage your website to incorporate a majority of your affiliate links. Currently, why is this of utmost importance? As an affiliate, you will be provided with an affiliate link for each product. It is essential that your prospects click on your specific affiliate link in order for any purchases they make to be attributed to your account.

Affiliate links serve as the means by which the affiliate network is informed of the appropriate commission allocation. Given that you will be overseeing a multitude of products, you will be endowed with a commensurate amount of affiliate links. This could potentially be highly unreliable. If you intend to promote them individually, please note that each one will necessitate its own dedicated campaign.

Regardless...

If you possess a website, you can establish a paramount campaign to direct your prospective customers to your central headquarters, where all your affiliate links can be accessed. Everything will be concentrated. Everything will be simpler. "When you have made the decision to construct your website, there are two essential requirements that you will need: OR "Once you have opted to establish your website, the process necessitates the fulfillment of two fundamental prerequisites:

a domain name; and

a hosting account

Your domain name serves as your digital address on the World Wide Web. "When selecting a domain name for your affiliate marketing campaign, kindly consider the following guidelines:

The selection of a domain name should align with the specific industry or field in which you are engaged.

The domain name should be easily memorable.

The designation of the locality should possess an alluring quality.

To the greatest extent possible, choose the domain extension ".com," or if it is no longer available, opt for ".org" or ".net." These extensions are widely recognized and easily memorable to people.

Additionally, you will need to procure a hosting account. The most suitable suggestion that I can propose is www.hostgator.com, which boasts a comprehensive range of services to meet all the requirements of your online business. Examine it firsthand to ascertain its content and purpose.

Essentially, you should be seeking three key factors from the hosting service you are evaluating. These are:

Storage domain refers to the capacity for storing a specific quantity of records within a given record system. Do not settle for anything less than a minimum of 50mb.

The bandwidth capacity threshold refers to the maximum level of information exchange that can be accommodated by the web hosting service. Do not settle for anything less than a monthly allocation of 15GB.

- Exceptional specialized assistance - your website serves as a valuable business ally. - Superb specialized support - your website acts as a strategic business partner. - Outstanding technical assistance - your website functions as a trusted business associate. - Exceptional specialized aid - your website serves as a reliable business companion. - Remarkable technical support - your website acts as a vital business collaborator. It is imperative that it remains operational at all times. In the event of a website outage, it is imperative that the hosting service promptly provides support to restore its availability, as the viability of your business relies upon it.

In addition, it will be necessary for you to have an autoresponder service. The matter of utmost significance that we will thoroughly delve into in the following section pertains to email marketing. Essentially, a significant portion of your success will hinge upon the size and level of engagement of your mailing list.

What's that? "Mailing list?" you ask?

Indeed, it will be necessary to construct a mailing list in order to convert uninterested onlookers into potential customers. Indeed, it is factual that your deals will stem from the prospects you generate. Additionally, what renders email marketing feasible is the acquisition of a subscription to an autoresponder service. I assure you that investing in an autoresponder service is one of the most crucial steps on your path to achieving success in affiliate marketing. It is essential that you carefully select a reputable autoresponder service that will offer you a solid foundation on which to build.

I would recommend considering Aweber.com, which is widely regarded as the most superior autoresponder service currently available on the market. Procure an affiliate membership promptly, should you desire to do so, because in the future, you will realize the utmost importance it holds for enhancing your affiliate marketing endeavors.

Having acquired the majority of this information, the process of creating a website should be straightforward. If you possess fundamental knowledge of HTML programming, then tasks will prove to be even more manageable. Should you not possess the necessary expertise, rest assured that there are several WYSIWYG HTML editors available for your convenience. In the event that you require a simpler alternative, you can readily establish a complimentary WordPress account and initiate the construction of your website via Wordpress.com.

4. SELECTING A DOMAIN NAME

The selection of a domain is not considered as important when it comes to constructing an affiliate niche website. A long-standing discussion pertains to the decision between opting for an expired domain or a fresh domain when it comes to selecting a domain name.

The domain that I selected for my website was a previously expired domain that provided me with a competitive advantage in terms of article rankings. Nevertheless, this does not imply that new domains are any less perilous. Many individuals, nonetheless, suffer significant losses when it comes to purchasing expired domains, with even prominent industry marketer Neil Patel unable to salvage the situation.

There are several factors that must be taken into account if you are opting for the route of expired domains: The primary advantage of possessing an expired domain is the inherent benefit of having multiple sites linking to your domain, which provides significant search engine optimization value to expedite the ranking of your website.

Would you like to acquire information regarding the purchasing of expired domain names? Please refer to the detailed guides provided at these locations: here and here. Please be advised to exercise caution and perform thorough background checks prior to finalizing a domain name for your website.

However, I would strongly recommend against pursuing the option of acquiring expired domains, as genuine ones can command prices in the range of hundreds of dollars, while only the low-quality, spam-ridden domains are available at a lower cost. Presently, one may inquire about the status of recently obtained domain names.

Acquiring brand new domain names is akin to acquiring a pristine automobile, whereby you are aware that you will be the initial proprietor, with no involvement from any other party.

It can be beneficial for individuals who are new to this process and wish to prevent potential mishaps when selecting an expired domain. Despite the recent establishment of your domain, you can achieve both high search engine rankings and financial success from your website within a relatively short timeframe of 3-4 months.

Therefore, refrain from contemplating expired domains. If you are unable to locate a satisfactory one within a day, it is advisable to reserve a current domain instead. Moving on. Now that we have completed the domain name acquisition process, let us now proceed to discuss the selection of the domain name itself.

Comparing Exact Match Domains and Partial Match Domains.

Let us consider the primary keyword I am focusing on: Best Self Balancing Scooter under 1000. Here is an example of an Exact Match Domain that could be used:

It is quite evident to anyone of discernment that EMD's possess an unsightly appearance, which can be deemed as highly unattractive. During a previous era of SEO, it was possible to achieve high rankings simply by utilizing an Exact Match Domain (EMD). However, those days have permanently passed.

Nowadays, the focus lies in establishing authority and a strong brand presence. If your domain appears unappealing, it is highly likely that your website's performance will be severely undermined.

Partially Matching Domains (PMDs), on the contrary, represent enhanced iterations of Exact Match Domains (EMDs), in which you incorporate solely one principal term or its synonym within your domain.

Therefore, in the event that the keyword I am focusing on is "Best Self Balancing Scooter under 1000," the domain I might consider selecting could potentially be scootharmony.com or symmetryscooter.com instead.

I must acknowledge the unconventional appearance of the domain names, as I struggled to generate suitable alternatives within the limited time frame. However, this approach enables me to construct a name that is concise, highly memorable, and easily entered by users into their web browsers.

By utilizing this indispensable guide, you will successfully formulate a captivating and distinctive domain name.

The main objective at hand is to achieve a harmonious equilibrium in the selection of a domain that can readily establish a brand presence, be it through the choice of a new domain or the pursuit of expired domains.

5. PROVISION AND CONFIGURATION OF HOSTING SERVICES AND WEBSITE SETUP

Once you have thoroughly explored a well-researched niche and secured a highly valuable domain, it is imperative to obtain a hosting service capable of effectively managing your website.

What type of hosting do you require?

Based on your technical expertise, you have two alternatives when selecting hosting for your specialized website.

Choosing between Shared Hosting or Cloud VPS plans.

I highly endorse considering Hostgator.com (while avoiding Hostgator.in) or Interserver.net for Shared Hosting, as they offer one of the most dependable hosting services I have personally encountered.

Please take note that the coupon code '1cent1month' can be utilized when signing up with Interserver.net to avail the first month of hosting at a cost of $0.01. It is worth noting that DigitalOcean is widely regarded as the top choice for cloud VPS hosting. Discouraged for beginners, though I have already composed a comprehensive manual on the process of establishing a WordPress website on DigitalOcean. You may refer to it at your convenience.

There is an ongoing and substantial debate regarding the decision to opt for either Shared Hosting or Cloud VPS hosting. Nevertheless, I would recommend selecting it based on your proficiency.

If you are a newcomer, Shared Hosting proves to be an excellent choice. However, if you are already familiar with the issues associated with Shared Hosting, opting for the VPS route can be considered a viable alternative.

Selection of Theme and Establishment of the Website

I have been the recipient of countless acknowledgments from fellow bloggers for the design and theme that I carefully selected for my specialized website.

Selecting a theme encompasses more than mere visual appeal and ornate features. It pertains to the velocity at which content is loaded and the effective implementation of SEO optimization.

Nevertheless, that does not imply that you should select a theme that is uninteresting and appears to have been created in the early 2000s. To be direct and concise, I highly recommend the utilization of the Schema theme available from MyThemeShop.com. This particular theme offers the ability to customize its appearance according to your preferences. Additionally, it boasts exceptional SEO optimization, fast loading speed, and the inclusion of Schema markup. This advantageous combination provides you with a significant competitive advantage over your rivals.

If you are not aligned with the Schema theme, it is worth considering themes offered by developers such as Thrive Themes and Studiopress.

Once you have selected the theme of your preference. Please consult this guide for the purpose of configuring your website in under 20 minutes.

Elevate Affiliate Marketing As Your Primary Source Of Income

The primary source of income for the majority of bloggers stems from affiliate marketing and the resulting commissions. Affiliate marketing is effective for bloggers as their readers visit their blogs seeking reliable evaluations and information pertaining to various products and services accessible.

Given the vast array of information available on the Internet, selecting the specific product or service on which to allocate one's hard-earned funds can pose a considerable challenge. Bloggers and affiliate marketing form a harmonious partnership, as they unite products that resonate with bloggers and appeal to their readers, while simultaneously generating revenue through product sales.

In numerous instances, bloggers may not be required to engage in any additional action beyond embedding a hyperlink within the body of their articles. This hyperlink will monitor the occurrence of user clicks and assess whether or not an individual completes a purchase transaction. The customers are not required to make an immediate purchase as the blogger will receive the commission if the customer eventually decides to make the purchase at a later time. This is made possible through the use of cookies in affiliate marketing, which store information about when and where the product was initially clicked on.

What precisely is the concept of affiliate marketing?

Affiliate marketing pertains to the establishment of connections among advertisers, publishers, and consumers with the aim of generating sales. The advertiser usually possesses a product or service for sale but requires assistance in the process of selling it. The advertiser will seek assistance from a publisher to disseminate their message and establish a connection with consumers, and they are willing to compensate the publisher for this service.

A publisher is an individual who conveys the advertiser's message to the consumer through the use of a link, banner ad, or an email newsletter. The consumer perceives the message and will take action by selecting the link, advertisement, or newsletter, thereby redirecting them from the publisher's website to the advertiser's website. The ultimate stage occurs when the customer engages in a purchase, thus accomplishing the action, which is referred to as a conversion.

How does the process of affiliate marketing operate?

The advertiser will provide the publisher with a distinct identification number for each of their websites to monitor and handle each individual click. Monitoring the individual click counts for each product is the method through which the publisher receives commission from affiliate marketing.

In addition to the publisher receiving a unique identifier, each product or link utilized by the publisher is also assigned its own distinct identification. The integration of distinct identifiers for both the publisher's website and the product enables the monitoring of consumer behavior. If a consumer engages with an affiliate marketing hyperlink, cookies will allow the affiliate marketer to retain information concerning the date, time, and location (website) of the consumer's interaction with the hyperlink. Enabling cookies permits the website to discern whether the consumer revisits at a subsequent time to make a purchase, thereby finalizing the conversion.

This is the point at which the publisher will be entitled to receive a commission based on the sale. The affiliate network is an enterprise that manages the connections between advertisers and publishers, establishing a consortium of other entities that utilize their platform.

Why Use Affiliate Marketing?

Affiliate marketing presents the most convenient method for monetizing your website. To become a member of an affiliate marketing website, it is necessary to register by creating an account and unique ID. Subsequently, one should proceed to search for products to integrate into their website, and then proceed to paste the corresponding links onto their site. After this, one can patiently await the arrival of compensation.

The hyperlinks may be presented as either text or visuals, or a combination of both, depending on the requirements of your website. Although this is the most straightforward method, there are certain strategies that will be addressed in the following chapter in order to assist you in becoming a prosperous affiliate marketer.

Affiliate marketing serves as the optimal method for advertisers to effectively establish connections with consumers, and as the publisher, you are their crucial element. In your role as a publisher, your readers place their trust in your discernment. As a result, when you offer them a recommendation, they frequently pay heed and act accordingly.

You hold significant value to advertisers, and you can leverage this to your benefit when seeking to monetize your website. To clarify, it should be noted that you are the affiliate marketer. The advertisers and publishers are collaborating in order to mutually generate profit; without each other, there would be no financial gain to be accrued.

Using your email mailing list is an optimal method for disseminating affiliate marketing messages to your readers. Frequently, individuals may not discern or express concern regarding your inclusion of a hyperlink directing them to a website for the purpose of acquiring the product. In fact, in many instances, your reader will be gratified by the presence of the link.

In contrast to advertisements that frequently go unnoticed or make consumers feel targeted, affiliate marketing links prove advantageous to the consumer. Affiliate marketing proves highly advantageous for consolidating multiple hyperlinks within a single article or webpage. Each affiliate marketing network will offer an extensive range of products to meticulously explore, ensuring the ideal match for your website's specific niche.

While incorporating numerous links to optimize your earning potential, there are instances when prioritizing quality over quantity is crucial. Do exercise caution when including an excessive number of products without considering their potential benefit to your readers. The presence of numerous links in your articles may prove bothersome to your audience, possibly leading to a diminished opinion of your website.

Incorporating affiliate marketing on your website is straightforward, user-friendly, and employs a transparent approach to monetizing your site. You solely provide endorsements for various products on your website and that is the extent of it. It's highly advantageous as it relieves the burden of product creation and ensuring its delivery to the customer. All one needs to do is promote it on their website and delegate the responsibility of the remaining operations to the advertisers.